First published in the U.K. 1983 by Blandford Press,
Link House, West Street, Poole, Dorset, BH15 1LL

Copyright © 1983 Blandford Books Ltd

Based on Blandford's original Very First Bible Stories,
illustrated by Treyer Evans, and others.

Co-edition arranged with the help of Angus Hudson, London.

ISBN 0 7137 1321 6

Made and printed in Italy

Baby Jesus

By Dorothy Allen

Illustrated by Patricia Papps
and Andrew Skilleter

BLANDFORD PRESS

Poole   Dorset

Here is Mary, standing by the window. The Angel Gabriel has come to see her to give her a message. "Mary," he says, "God is going to give you a baby boy, and you must call Him Jesus."

Mary and Joseph are in their little home at Nazareth. Mary is sewing. They are very happy thinking about the baby that is soon to be born.

Mary and Joseph have to leave their home for a while as everyone has to go to his own town to have his name recorded. They are going to Bethlehem because it is Joseph's town. Mary is riding a donkey and Joseph is leading it.

Now Mary and Joseph have come to Bethlehem. It is evening and already getting dark.

They are looking for somewhere to sleep, but they cannot find anywhere because all the houses are full of people.

They stop at many houses to ask if there is any room for them, but there is none.

At last, one man says, "I am sorry I have no room for you in the house, but you can sleep in the stable, if you like."

So Mary and Joseph go into the stable where the cows and other animals sleep. It is dark inside, but Joseph has a lantern, so they can see.

Poor Mary! She is feeling so tired now. Joseph has unpacked something to eat and they are sitting on the straw to have their supper. Then they will settle down to sleep.

Very early next morning, while it is still dark, Baby Jesus is born. Here He is in His mummy's arms. Mary is feeling so happy because she has a baby now. She has wrapped Him up warmly.

Mary has no proper cot for Baby Jesus so she puts Him in a manger, where the hay is fed to the cows.

Out in the fields shepherds are looking after their sheep. It is very early in the morning.

Suddenly, a bright light shines around them and an angel appears.

"Don't be afraid," he says. "I have come to tell you something that will make everyone happy. A baby called Jesus has just been born in Bethlehem. You will find Him in a stable, lying in a manger."

23

Then the shepherds see many angels and they hear them singing to God in praise.

Soon the angels have gone, and the shepherds are alone with their sheep. They say to each other, "Let us go to Bethlehem and find Baby Jesus."

So off they go. They leave their sheep for a while and start along the road to Bethlehem. It is getting light now and the sun will soon be up.

Here are the shepherds in the stable. They have found Baby Jesus and here He is in His mummy's arms. The shepherds love Jesus and are so pleased to see Him. One of them has brought a little lamb with him to see Baby Jesus too.

29

The shepherds have said goodbye to Baby Jesus. Now they are telling everyone that they have seen Him, and all the people are so pleased to hear about Him.

It is morning now and the sun is shining. The shepherds are going back to look after their sheep. On the way they sing because they are so happy, and they thank God for Baby Jesus.

Another day, more people come to see Baby Jesus. They are three wise men, riding on camels, who have come from afar to see him.

They are following a bright star in the sky which is showing them the way to Baby Jesus.

The three wise men have come into the house. Now they can see Baby Jesus. They are kneeling down in front of Him, and have brought Him presents. The first one has brought gold. The second has brought perfume. And the third has brought sweet-smelling ointment.

Now the wise men are saying goodbye to Baby Jesus. They have to return to their own country.

On Christmas Day we specially think of Baby Jesus, because it is His birthday. It is the most wonderful birthday of all. We give each other presents, and try to make everyone happy.

Here are lots of children looking at Baby Jesus. They have come to see Him because they love Him very much.